T0070773

THE ISLE OF
ORLEANS

B♭ TRUMPET
SOLO

MUSIC MINUS ONE

3850

SUGGESTIONS FOR USING THIS MMO EDITION

WE HAVE TRIED to create a product that will provide you an easy way to learn and perform these compositions with a full ensemble in the comfort of your own home. Because it involves a fixed accompaniment performance, there is an inherent lack of flexibility in tempo. The following MMO features and techniques will reduce these inflexibilities and help you maximize the effectiveness of the MMO practice and performance system:

We have observed generally accepted tempi, and always in the originally intended key, but some may wish to perform at a different tempo, or to slow down or speed up the accompaniment for practice purposes; or to alter the piece to a more comfortable key. We have included slow-tempo versions of the most up-tempo pieces on this album for practice and/or a slower interpretation. But for even more flexibility, you can purchase from MMO specialized CD players & recorders which allow variable speed while maintaining proper pitch, and vice versa. This is an indispensable tool for the serious musician and you may wish to look into purchasing this useful piece of equipment for full enjoyment of all your MMO editions.

We want to provide you with the most useful practice and performance accompaniments possible. If you have any suggestions for improving the MMO system, please feel free to contact us. You can reach us by e-mail at info@musicminusone.com.

CONTENTS

3850

©2004 MMO Music Group, Inc. All rights reserved.
ISBN 1-59615-104-8

Bb Trumpet

Magnolia Dance

Tim Laughlin

©2003 Tim Laughlin Music BMI. International Copyrights Secured. All Rights Reserved. Used by permission.

Bb Trumpet

Restless Heart

Tim Laughlin

©2003 Tim Laughlin Music BMI. International Copyrights Secured.
All Rights Reserved. Used by permission.

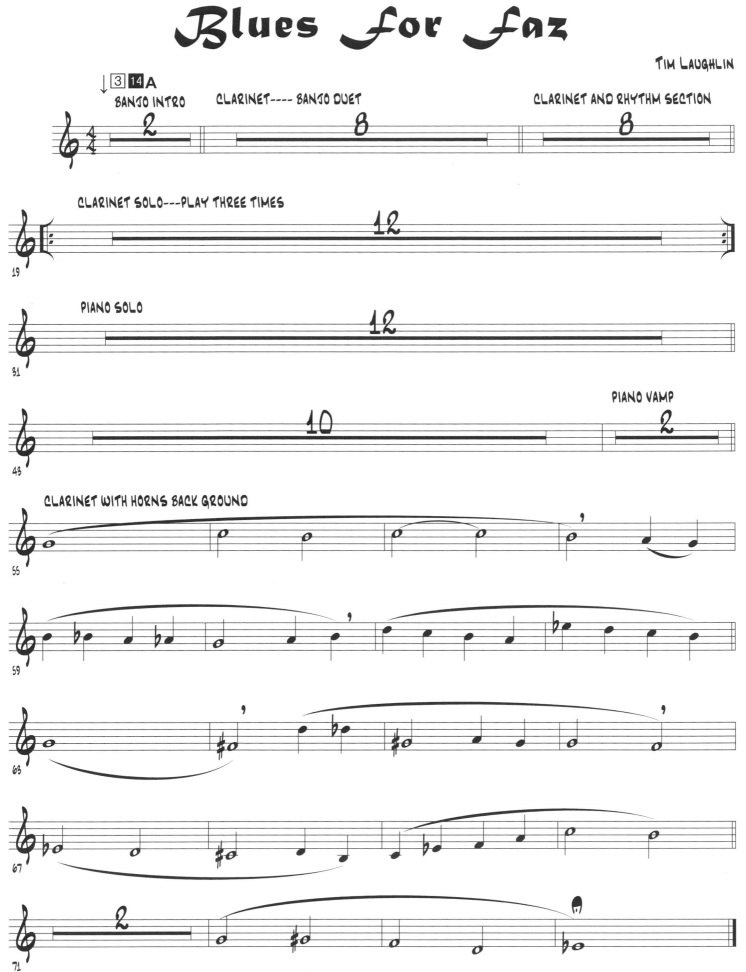

©2003 Tim Laughlin Music BMI. International Copyrights Secured. All Rights Reserved. Used by permission.

MMO 3850

Suburban St. Parade

Tim Laughlin

DRUM SOLO

Pick-ups

DIXIELAND BAND ENSEMBLE-=--PLAY TWO TIMES

CLARINET SOLO
TWO TIMES

CORNET SOLO

©2003 Tim Laughlin Music BMI. International Copyrights Secured.
All Rights Reserved. Used by permission.

Bb Trumpet

It's My Love Song To You

Tim Laughlin

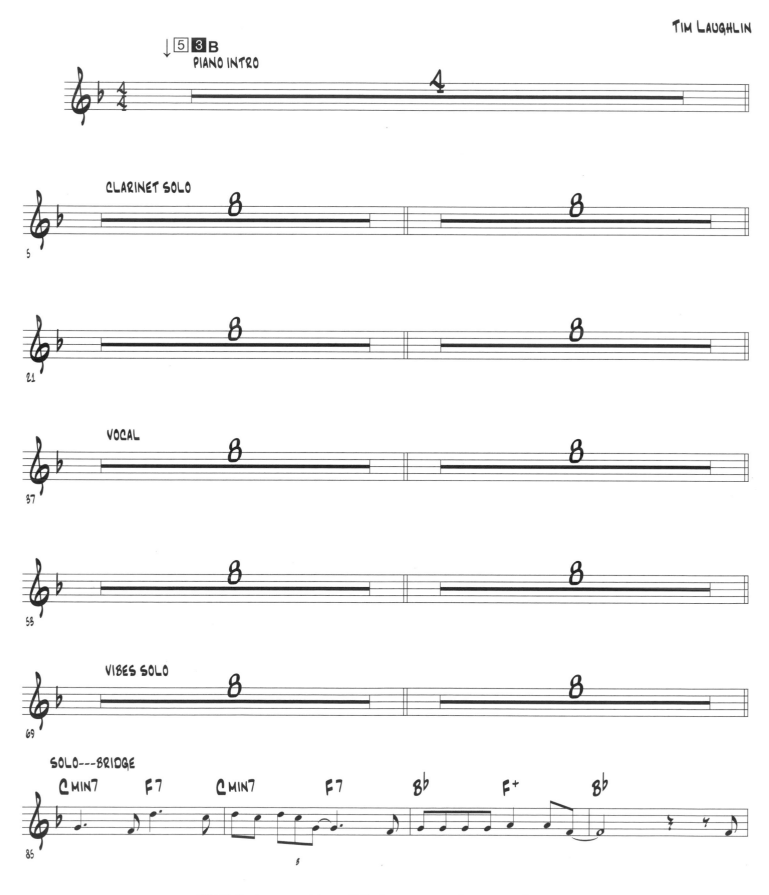

©2003 Tim Laughlin Music BMI. International Copyrights Secured.
All Rights Reserved. Used by Permission.

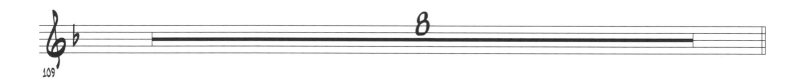

Bb Trumpet

Gentilly Strut

Tim Laughlin

©2003 Tim Laughlin Music BMI. International Copyrights Secured.
All Rights Reserved. Used by permission.

Bb TRUMPET

I Know I'll See You Again

Tim Laughlin

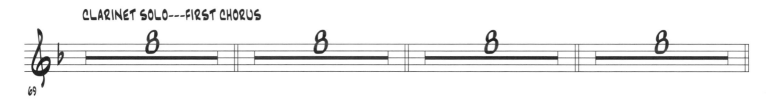

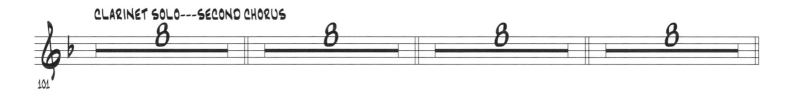

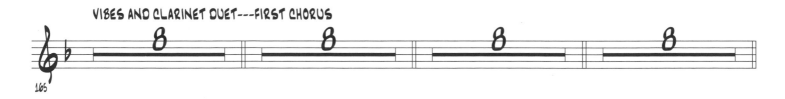

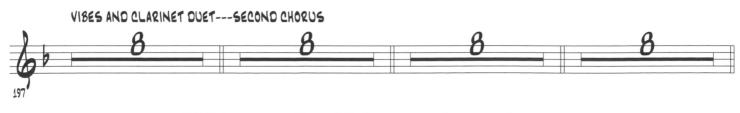

©2003 Tim Laughlin Music BMI. International Copyrights Secured.
All Rights Reserved. Used by permission.

DIXIELAND ENSEMBLE---PLAY TWO TIMES

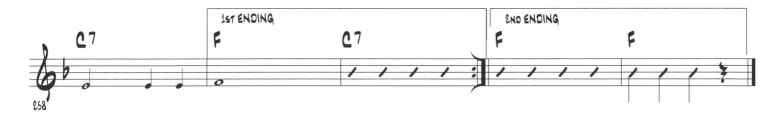

Bb Clarinet

Crescent City Moon

Tim Laughlin

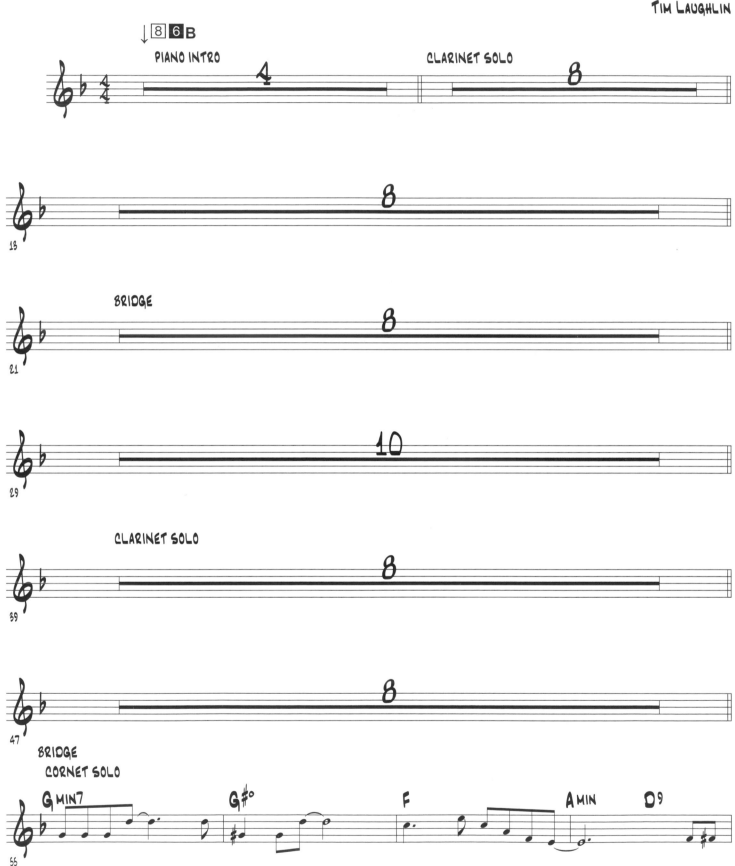

©2003 Tim Laughlin Music BMI. International Copyrights Secured. All Rights Reserved. Used by permission.

Bb Trumpet

The Isle of Orleans

Tim Laughlin

©2003 Tim Laughlin Music BMI. International Copyrights Secured. All Rights Reserved. Used by permission.

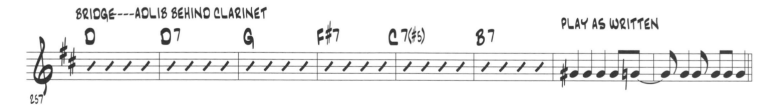

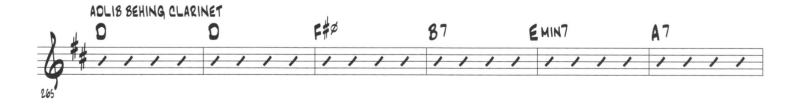

Monkey Hill

Tim Laughlin

©2003 Tim Laughlin Music BMI. International Copyrights Secured.
All Rights Reserved. Used by permission.

23

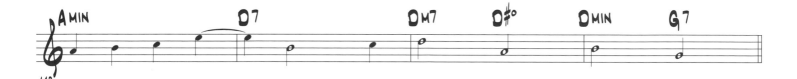

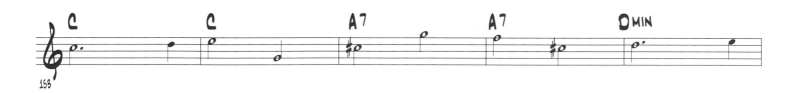

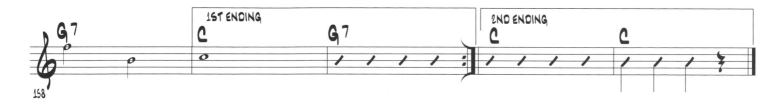

MUSIC MINUS ONE
50 Executive Boulevard
Elmsford, New York 10523-1325
1.800.669.7464 (U.S.)/914.592.1188 (International)

www.musicminusone.com
e-mail: mmogroup@musicminusone.com